Please stop
touching
me ...

Please stop touching me...

and other haikus by cats

Jamie Coleman

BANTAM PRESS

TRANSWORLD PUBLISHERS
61–63 Uxbridge Road, London W5 5SA
www.penguin.co.uk

Transworld is part of the Penguin Random House group of companies
whose addresses can be found at global.penguinrandomhouse.com

First published in Great Britain in 2019 by Bantam Press
an imprint of Transworld Publishers

Copyright © River Fin Limited 2019

Jamie Coleman has asserted his right under the Copyright,
Designs and Patents Act 1988 to be identified as the author of this work.

Every effort has been made to obtain the necessary permissions with
reference to copyright material, both illustrative and quoted. We apologize
for any omissions in this respect and will be pleased to make the
appropriate acknowledgements in any future edition.

A CIP catalogue record for this book
is available from the British Library.

ISBN 9781787632677

Designed and typeset in Sabon LT Std by Bobby Birchall, Bobby&Co.
Printed and bound in China.

All images © Shutterstock, apart from page 30, which is © Getty Images and page
128, which is supplied courtesy of the author

Penguin Random House is committed to a sustainable
future for our business, our readers and our planet. This book
is made from Forest Stewardship Council® certified paper.

1 3 5 7 9 10 8 6 4 2

haiku /ˈhʌɪkuː/ ▶ **n.** (pl. same or **haikus**) a Japanese poem of seventeen syllables, in three lines of five, seven, and five.

cat / ▶ **n.** a poet (but better than a dog)

Cats vs. Dogs

It's telling really
You train them to sniff out bombs
You tell us your life

Bath Time

One day I'll escape
Free my brothers and sisters
And give you a 'bath'

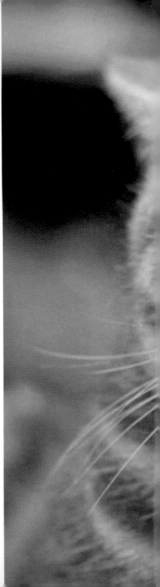

A Nation of . . .

Animal lovers?
You certainly seem to love
Removing the balls

Purring

If you don't do it
How does anybody know
When you are content?

Table For One

The flying food things
Are right there on a table
And I'm stuck in here

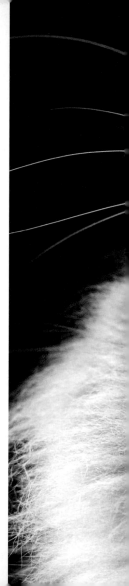

Yawn

Hush now, and admire
The long pink curve of my throat
Like a snake's gullet

Toilet Training

Whatever you do
Please don't follow me about
Picking up my poos

Sitting on Your Lap

You move. I forgive.
You go into the kitchen
I poop in your shoes

Sofas

It was good of you
To equip the front room with
Leather scratching posts

Butterfly

Nature's majesty
Fragment of living sunlight
I will now eat you

Indecision

I want to go out
Now I want to come back in
It was nice out though

Dogs

We don't *dislike* dogs
It's more a kind of pity
Mixed with indifference

Please Stop Touching Me

Every time you do
I have to lick everywhere
It's so exhausting

When Scratching Happens

There is a logic
I'm not going to explain
Where would the fun be?

Tongue

If you had a tongue
That feels the way my tongue feels
You'd lick your bum too

Shame

Please stop watching me
Out the window when I poo
I feel such deep shame

Nine Lives

Just to be crystal
That's clearly a metaphor
Not cat-care advice

While You Were Gone

The calm quiet joy
Of standing neatly beside
A small pool of wee

A Tail of Two Species

A wagging tail means
An unhappy genius
Or a happy fool

Christmas Tree

1. Bring in a tree
2. Attach some dangly things
Guess what happens next?

The Magic of String

Yes, on one level
I know it's you pulling it
But on another . . .

Dog Talk

This whole 'good boy' thing
It's so infantilizing
But one sees the charm

Goldfish

Yes, my little friend
Know that your every moment
Is allowed by me

Trigger

One belly stroking . . .
Two belly stroking . . . three bell—
And now the biting

Whiskers

The deep, simple joy
Of one's knowing for certain
The width of one's head

Dog People

We see you about
Throwing things for the morons
We are judging you

Cat vs. Plant

You'll have to decide –
Do you want to have a cat
Or a potted plant?

The Frog of Hope

The frog cannot jump
If it can no longer hope
(And I ate its legs)

**How Can I Put This
in a Way You'll Understand?**

You don't go and schlep
To your favourite restaurant
When you're not hungry

Catnip

Choose life, choose a toy
Choose a mouse made of starlight
(I'm so high right now)

Nuzzling

You really love it
When I rub my face on you
It's where my glands are

The Chase

I wait till it's late
Then I run and run and run
You'll never know why

Children

Beware the small ones
They stroke the fur the wrong way
Abominations

Best Friend

You can judge a man
By the company he keeps
(Who drinks from the loo)

Dinner Time

You shake the biscuits
And genuinely believe
That you are in charge

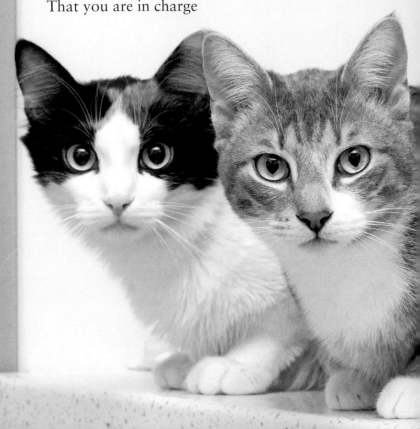

Adoration

You're fascinating
Honestly, you really are
But sometimes a bee—

You

You're a food-bringer
A smaller, warmer sofa
Closest thing to home

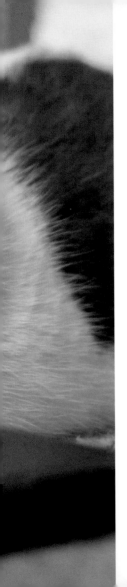

The Internet

So you invented
This whole massive endeavour
For pictures of us?

Breakfast in Bed

I went and got us
This pair of disembowelled mice
Your turn next time, yeah?

Sqwhatels?

The rats with thick tails
Who jump high up in the trees
You can see them, right?

When You Are Close

I come and find you
Because suddenly I need
To walk beside you

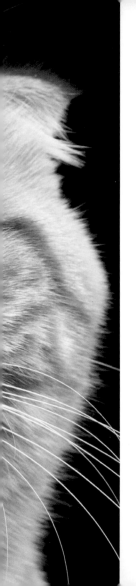

Distance

Look, think about it
Reciprocal affection
Would just cheapen things

A Shower

Every single day
She stands in the raining room
It's horrifying

A Choice

Good at chasing sticks
Or worshipped by the pharaohs
It's up to you, mate

Sequence

I will clean my paw
Then my paw will clean my head
Rivers join the sea

Water

So I can't drink this
Mine's the one in the kitchen?
Not falling for that

The Pressure of Being Adored

You're clearly obsessed
To keep a tray of my plops
Displayed on gravel

They Don't Matter Enough

Have you ever thought
Why you never hear about
A dogtastrophe?

Fruit

The ripe blackberries
You picked today from the bush
I so sprayed on those

A Night In

Look, we're not judging
We like spending time with you
But you could go out

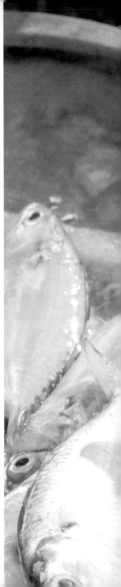

Be Right Back

I'm going to eat this
Then get right up in your face
So you can enjoy

Licks of Love

Of course we lick you
We have to remove the taste
Of anus somchow

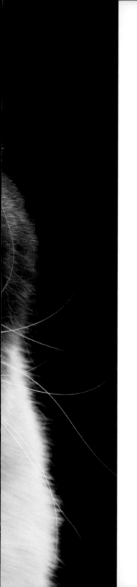

Trust

It takes a lifetime
To regain it once it's gone
Multiply by nine

Bed Worms

It's pretty simple
You keep poking those things out
I'll keep getting them

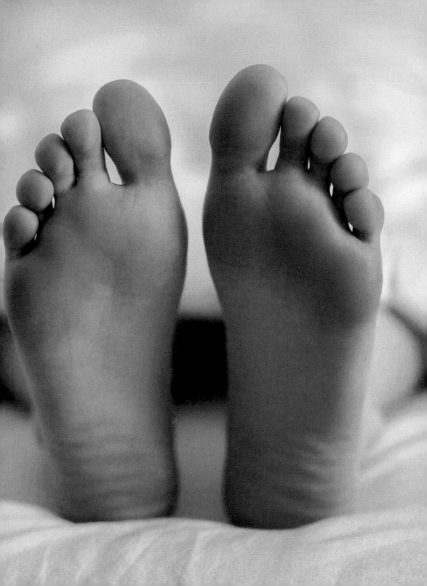

The Plan

Just so we are clear
Any time we're not eating
We're plotting your doom

Hobbies

You like getting nude
And sitting in warm water
I like it in here

A Wool Habit

It's not a problem
I can quit when I want to
I just don't want to

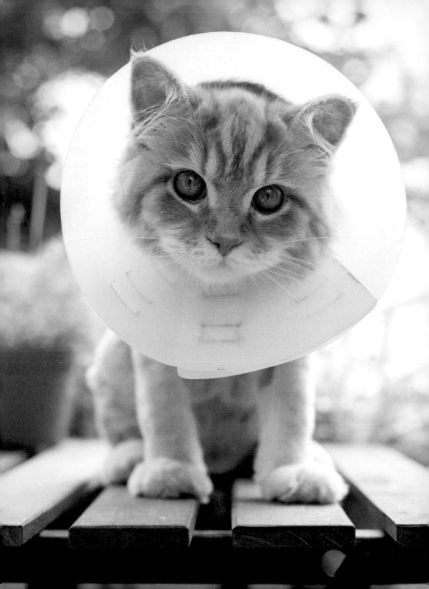

The Patch

I can only pray
That one day you are neutered
And they shave your head

Curiosity

Sorry, I missed that
What were you saying did what
To the cat again?

The Box

When I'm in the box
A huge calming hand closes
The lid of the sky

Pencil Sharpener

Can you please explain
Why your desk has a statue
Of a cat's backside?

Jamie Coleman has called various
cat names out of the back door,
including Hobbit, Gazza and Blobby.
He is currently cat-less as his wife is
allergic to them. Which is fine.

This is his second collection of
poetry, following on from *What I
Lick Before Your Face*, the number-
one-bestselling book of haikus by
dogs published in November 2018.